LIVE *Life* OF YOUR *Dreams*

LIVE *Life* OF YOUR *Dreams*

Dr. Anita Moral

PARTRIDGE

To order additional copies of this book, contact
Partridge India
000 800 10062 62
orders.india@partridgepublishing.com

www.partridgepublishing.com/india

Contents

This book is dedicated to my parents, and those lionhearted souls who fall again and again but stand each time with more courage and strength with full determination to achieve winning in life.

Acknowledgements

Words will be less to express my sense of gratitude towards 'Almighty', who has bestowed me the highest luxury "As Human Life ".

So, I acknowledge first of all you 'God', without whom it would not be possible for me to understand and comprehend the hidden lessons behind challenges in life. So I express my first word of gratitude to you 'Almighty'.

Further, I am especially thankful to the extraordinary people in my life, I have blessed with, who always keep their utter faith in me, that's why it is only possible today, I am helping people to understand and comprehend their own challenges in life. I am thankful to all those incredible people in my life who helped me to recognize my ideas and then in shaping them. I am heartily thankful for their encouragements and trust in me.

Further, I express my thanks to the entire team of 'Partridge Penguin India' which has been so supportive of my work and for my idea of publish with Partridge Penguin. Thanks to Yaneesa Evans, Marry Oxley, Kathy Lorenzo, Pearl Jade and the whole Partridge team who helped me directly or indirectly for keeping my things before you as an author.

My acknowledgements can never be complete without mentioning my family who has encouraged me from the day one. I am so much thankful to my 'MA' and 'PA', who are my ever source inspiration and whose kind wisdom has shaped my life. I also offer my thanks to my lovable brothers(Devisaran, Deepak Saran) , I especially pay my gratitude to Deepak Saran whose motivational conversations work like a torch bearer for me , and whose own journey of life proves and validates the techniques , I have discussed in the book. Love you lot my little champion. I also can't forget to express my thanks to another chap (my brother) Vikas Bharti, who suggested me first among all to pile up my ideas and techniques in form of a book. I also must acknowledge to my sweet sister (Kavita) for her worthy discussions time to time and sister in law (Twinkle) for her cherishing and shared moments. Further, my acknowledgement can't be done without keeping the role of my sweet, witty, sparkling son 'Arudaya' whose spontaneity tells me, "how beautiful life is"! I also express my special gratitude to my sweetheart hubby (Dr. RajKumar Bajaj) for all your love and blessings you have brought in my life.

Lastly, I should say thanks to my readers, what I have written is written for you. I really feel fortunate to have the readers, trust in me. So I offer heartfelt thanks to each and every one of you for the belief you have in me.

An Introduction from Anita Moral

Who, in the world, don't want to live life of his/her dream; and how many are people living that life actually; take a pause and think! Think about your family, your friends, your surroundings and think about everyone you know. How many of them are living the life as they really want? Or how many are enjoying the life, they have got?

I believe, you have track the answer; whether the answer is on any side if people are living life of their dreams or not, it's not your point. The point to be noticed here by you is:

Why some people are living life of their dream?

And why some are suffering for the same?

The present book "Live Life of Your Dreams" will create an insight within you to know the answer of these questions.

People have individual differences, it can't be avoided. So the kind of their achievement and success is different, their criterion for happiness is different.

The reason behind their success and happiness is different. But, Regardless of all these differences one thing is same and that is the showering of universe. People are different to each other but still the nature is distributing its disasters and blessings equally to everyone. If it is rain at some place, it is for everybody whether men or women, rich or poor, sane or insane, lazy or actives, intelligent or disabled, the raining will be same for everybody.

The difference lies here only, how you are able to keep you safe from harmful effects of rain. That is the same with success, achievement, happiness and miseries in life. Everyone gets success because of different factors and reasons, some because of hard work, some because of personal attitude towards life and some because of many other reasons.

But one thing is certain about each and every success and misery in life, and that is the law of universe, which is equal for everybody, but depends how you access these laws of nature, and this access is not possible without knowing the accessibility of your mind.

You are far bigger than you and others know about you. You can have everything in your life, of your desires. You just simply need to do some inner work for you with some certain techniques or laws for success and happiness in life.

The pages of the book will reveal you these beautiful laws precisely and will surely inspire you to practice them all, as the ring in your fingers. "Live Life of Your Dreams" is a book about the 'Effects and Importance', Practice and Live" the techniques which are highly followed by the happy & successful people all around the world whether consciously or unconsciously.

As you go through the pages you will enjoy them one by one. I have tried to pour my all heart and mind onto these pages and shared all I know about, life of happiness, life of your choice, and finally how to live life of your dreams.

I am a human; I have my own limitations, struggles and inside wars. But still I am on progress along the way. I see myself a better person day by day from ancient years, because I continually challenge myself for a better day on each day. I want to break the myth that these kinds of books are only written by already enlightened beings.

No, this is never so, we all are human being, we have our own challenges, weaknesses and strengths. Every Single one of us has a bright and dark side; every single one of us has flaws and cries.

We all are human that's why imperfections but the whole journey of life on earth becomes incredible if learning and constant growth takes place due to these imperfections.

The pages of the book will reveal how to reach to perfections, obviously from imperfections.

Dr. Anita Moral

The all different mental techniques depicted in the book are very real and astoundingly powerful. If you choose to play with them, authentically you will start to live life of your dreams. I thank you all humbly, for having this book and for making it part of your life. I pay great honor and love for you for spending precious hours of your time in reading this book. I am sure the book will be a 'Priceless Jewel' in the incredulous account of your life.

Lastly, I wish you great blessings for living the life of your dreams.

With love,

Dr. Anita Moral

Acknowledge Yourself

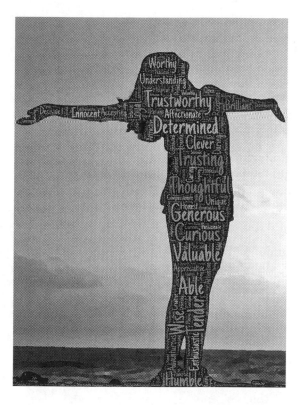

The quality of your vibrations determines your accomplishments. Whatever you elicit attracts the same in multiplications. So the old maxim that success attracts success, and 'money attracts money' is a great truth. Success vibration works like a magnet, attracts more success and opportunities to you.

This all happens because of the nature of your predominant thoughts. The people who are already on a momentum of success achieve more and more success due to their subliminal quality of thoughts. Physicists also say, 'Each thought radiates energy, and its frequency attracts the same type of frequency around you.' Therefore, 'success exceeds more success' and 'misery exceeds more misery.' But there are many reasons: mind often learns to remain in negative thoughts due to faulty learning patterns, rearing up techniques, some neurological reasons, and even by own critical inner voice. Some, more or less, negative experiences are frequently unavoidable, but reframing and reinterpretation is possible with a proactive mindset. Many mind lies within one mind. For example, one part of your mind can say, 'Tomorrow, I will start jogging early in the morning.' But when time comes to be awake for jogging, your another mind can say 'who cares for damn jogging?'

On a broad spectrum, there are two sides inside each one of us: one is the inner critic, and another is the inner protector.

Most of the time, this inner critic remains in continuous hammering to find faults with, or to find failures and inabilities. Even it magnifies small failures into big ones, punishes you with times over and over.

In the aura of this inner critic, you forget to give you credit for your good efforts. You even forget to listen to your inner protector.

The tendency of inner critic to remain on height and the inner protector to remain on low is the consequence of long trainings like faulty learning and parenting styles, conditionings, and all. Therefore, a deliberate shift is required to make the inner critic on low and to set up the inner protector on high. You need to stick up willingly with your inner protector so that you might be able to focus on your good qualities, to track your success area, to keep you on the road of brightness.

So that you can recondition you for a new perspective, for a new version of you, remember, acknowledgement of your mistakes is for new learning. Means you are not going to repeat them. You are becoming more aware and responsible.

For example, if you made fun of someone for his foolish act, sooner or later you might be aware that you exaggerated the point. At once your inner critic will take you in moral remorse, but if you are fully or deliberately aware with your inner protector, you will say that it was a casual gossip (which usually happen one or another), but is simply unskillful and need to be correct (never done again). This is the soft and sophisticated manner to keep you constant for new learning and responsibilities without being too harsh with you.

So finally, you can change or reprogram your mind by various powerful techniques. One of them is called 'acknowledge yourself'. Acknowledge yourself refers to 'value yourself', 'to feel a worth in you as a person.' This worth should be evaluated from intrinsic values rather than extrinsic ones. People validate you from your external achievements (academic performance, social image, physical appearance, and so forth). Ironically, you also evaluate your self-worth on the basis of these external accomplishments, which never gets end and even can't be fulfilled. These external achievements have no limits and have endless boundaries because these external achievements are the comparative degrees given by society or by your inner critical voice. You are always called an achiever when you are one up from someone. In this sense, 'the all can't be above average at the same time.'

Studies also say that evaluation of self-worth, depending on external accomplishments, is actually harmful for mental health. Such people tend to have more conflict, stress, anger, academic problems, and relationship wrangles. The real self-worth is to know you as 'who you are,' not as 'what you do.'

According to Dr Neff, there is always someone richer, more attractive, or successful than we are. When you compare your achievements with others, you lessen its value. There is always someone, or more than one, who is ahead of you in the same achievement area. This is like a situation as you are driving on the road. Certainly, you are ahead of many and more; and on the same time, many are ahead of you. The same situation occurs in life. Many people are ahead of you, and many are lower of you. So depends on you whether you want to enjoy your achievements to have a count of your success, or you prefer to be in worry comparing with the people higher of you. Being always on comparing mode will make you reluctant and unaware about your key strengths. You will lose the chance to analyze your doings for your accomplishments.

So choose a better option for you rather than comparing with the people around you in the same field. You can motivate yourself by autosuggestions to touch the heights of success like them. You can observe them, follow them, and you can sharpen your tact by modelling them. This new way to perceive the things will attract more and more success for you, it will fill you with positive faith about your strengths, and certainly one day you will reach to the epoch of success. So choose the right for you. Think and clasp that with all your positive strength.

How to Search Your Success Area

- The self-acknowledgement begins with the search of the areas in your life where you are already successful. This area may be related to any part of your life, or with any time of your life whether past, present, or future. The area may be related to personal life, professional life, or social life. If you are feeling tough to find such areas, try to focus more and more on the things. Focusing will make you enable to find such part of your life where you can easily acknowledge yourself. For example, you may start to search your success area in your relationships.

- Try to shift your mind on your relations one by one. For example, maybe you are a very obedient son, maybe you are a very loyal friend, maybe you are a caring brother/sister, maybe you are the loving parent; so certainly, there might have been an area where you score higher. Try to reach and find this area of your life.

- This technique to look everything sharply and keenly will certainly help to find you your success area. The same technique you can follow to find success areas in your professional life, in your social life, or in your personal life. Possibilities are there. You might have been a failure or depressed in many parts of your life, but trust that there might have been certainly a segment where you are the master. This segment just needs your soft attention. Albeit, it is covered with the dusty layers of your failures, but your soft effort to uncover these layers will shine this segment where you are already successful.

The predominant thoughts that arise from these fulfilled areas will elicit positive energy within you that will vibrate its frequency, therefore, attract the same level of frequencies for you. Hence, your success journey starts from this moment of acknowledging yourself.

How to Use Acknowledging Technique

Make your list of acknowledgements for you, which consist of one to ten or more attributes that make you feel successful about you.

- Spend your ten minutes every day on this list in reading your positive attributes.

- Let the thoughts be reaped into your conscious to subconscious.

No sooner, a positive attitude will shape and become your behaviour to attract the success for you. By focusing on your positive, you are building a strong bridge of success for you. Self-acknowledgement is vital for you, says Gregory Alford, MS Psy, founder of Accelerated Coaching & Consulting.

Self-acknowledgement is the strong tool or strategy through which you know yourself, your weaknesses, and strengths. It reaps a sense of responsibility within you. When you learn to own the responsibilities for your deeds, you become stronger, stable, and a well-equipped person.

For example, when you acknowledge yourself for any wrong action, that realization makes you strong and enables you to face the consequences of that action, so you will learn not to repeat such acts further in life. But if you resist for that particular act, you are stopping yourself to learn from the opportunities life is giving you. Resistance not only affects you, but also starts to affect your relationships, career, social, and personal life. Remember when you accept your faults, you grow more and become more stable. On the same process, when you acknowledge yourself for your achievements and take responsibility for that, the evoked sense of value fills you with immense self-confidence, worthiness, and a sense of farsightedness. So try to recognize your intrinsic values and worth.

How to Increase Your Self-Worth

By following the rules of CEAT, you can increase your level of self-worth:

1. **Be compassionate** – try to treat yourself with as kindness and love as you treat your loved ones and friends.

2. **Accept yourself** – don't be so harsh on yourself for failures or rejections. Try to accept yourself as you are in real. Acceptance will increase your level of contentment,

and automatically, you will start to grow the real you want for.

3. **Explore yourself** – this is one of the great strategies often practiced by all great people. Explore yourself means to know yourself from within. It's not only about to be aware of your strengths and weaknesses but also to provide you a golden chance for openness, for new changes, and for new opportunities. It is the extensive learning process or an inward journey about what next to next about you. This technique not only increases your focus and concentration, but also helps you to become calm, peaceful, and stable.

4. **Teach yourself** – teaching others is an art, but teaching yourself is a great fun. 'Mind is such a great privilege bestowed on you by God, which can be trained as in the ways as you want.' So teach yourself to conquer over your negative thought patterns by various techniques like autosuggestions, visualization, acknowledging yourself, guided self-instruction, and so forth.

Acknowledgements or validations are crucial to enjoy the beautiful journey of life, whether 'by others' or 'by you to you.' The importance of validation can easily be understood with the example of being in love. When you are in love, you receive so heartfelt and ecstatic validations by your beloved such as you are so beautiful, so attractive, so handsome, so thoughtful, so caring, all and all and all. Such endless recognitions make you feel so fulfilled, as on seventh cloud. In the same way, mind also act if you validate yourself by your own words of praise. These own words of recognition fill you with a high level of competency and contentment. So choose, from today, to acknowledge yourself for you deeds, irrespective of any circumstances.

'Be human with you, acknowledge and enjoy your achievements, and put a feel of proud on your shoulders.'

Check Your Thoughts

Thoughts are the mental activity within the mind that encoded in the pattern of language. According to National Science Foundation, an average brain produces about 50,000 thoughts per day. About 95 per cent of these thoughts are repeated daily, and this large area of repeated thoughts creates the mindset. Your quality of life depends on the quality of this mindset. If this mindset is filled with proactive and positive thoughts, life will be filled with desired results you want, otherwise, vice-versa. This mindset develops habit and then routine of your life. It directly influences the results of life. Thoughts include both the internal conversation and the external conversation. However, most of the time, people are not aware of these conversations. They are so recursive in behave that a willing effort only can recognize the pattern of these conversations.

Having conversation with self or with other is perfectly okay, everyone does it, but difference occurs due to the pattern or quality of these thoughts. If the quality of these thoughts is positive, then you will become higher in happiness and success. If the quality is negative, then you are surely going to crush your self-confidence and happiness in life. Psychologists almost talk about three types of thinking:

1. **Pathological thinking:** Pathological thoughts can't see themselves. These thoughts are directed by some emotions, and that emotion may be negative or positive both, so pathological thoughts are influenced by emotions. According to John Raithee, the term 'pathological' is used to designate thinking that is imbalanced by emotion. The only purpose of pathological thought is to justify those emotions, which are creating imbalance.

2. **Logical Thinking:** This type of thinking works without emotion. It works like computer. It is based on some technical rules, seeks conclusions, and it is completely objective. The turn take by person in this thinking

are completely right or wrong. The conclusions are predetermined and fix.

3. **Psychological Thinking:** This type of thinking can see itself. It can be evaluated easily because of its goal understanding.

For example:

• A: I want to understand 'why am I upset'?

• A: Because I have scored low in my exams.

• A: I want to score high, so I have to work hard.

• A: So now, I will focus more on my studies.

The above example is the layout of psychological thinking. It arrives you to a succinct understanding for the goal. But need a fine energy to proceed.

Why People Focus More on Negative

People become more focused on negative thoughts because it's the brain's nature to alert itself for potential harm. Once it starts for negative, it creates a constant loop or circle for negative thoughts. Consequently, it becomes the pattern. If not interrupted or controlled, that later on leads to many psychological and physical distress. Psychologists have divided this negative thinking loop in many types.

According to David Burns and other cognitive psychologists, the following patterns are labeled as negative thinking pattern:

(A) **Labeling** – labeling is a form of thinking in which a person attaches a negative label to self or to others. For example, rather than saying 'I made a mistake,' he/she would say 'I am a looser.'

The same with other, rather than saying 'Robin made the mistake,' he will say 'Robin is a fool, a clown.' Labeling is a pattern of all-or-nothing thinking. You see yourself completely bad or others the same. This type of thought pattern leaves a very little room for constructive communication.

(B) **Magnification** – this is called binocular style of thinking. It means that you often enlarge the positive attributes of others, but you shrink your own positive skills. Even your interpretation about self becomes like this:

    (i)   'Oh, I was lucky that's why it happened.'

    (ii) 'They were polite, so they were praising me.'

Both of the above examples show that a magnifier thinker discounts his/her own skills and over count the other's one.

(C) **Mental Filter** – this is a type of thinking pattern in which you become so focused on one aspect of situation, that you can't see even the reset scene of the situation.

You can understand it with a conversation here between a teacher and student:

Student: So you disliked my assignment.

Teacher: What do you mean by dislike? Just look the overall remark by me given to assignment, say, what is it?

Student: Good assignment.

Teacher: Then why you said I dislike it.

Student: Yeah, but you further said I did not put enough evidence, etc.

Above conversation is the fine example of mental filtration. The student is only focusing on one negative aspect of the evaluation, and discounting other positives. Such students will always be disappointed with their performance even when they ought to be proceeding on them.

(D) **Jumping to Conclusions** – this is a type of thinking when you continuously believe that you are able to predict what is going to happen and why when you certainly think that you are able to observe. What other thinks and will do?

In jumping to conclusion, you tend to attach one reason for some conclusion. For example:

   (i)   Believing people are talking about you.

(ii) Believing your boss is knowingly misbehaving you due to your earlier wrangle with him.

(iii) Believing your teacher is partial for you.

Jumping to conclusion means judgmental bias without knowing the proof, and without having enough information to be sure they are right. This type of thought pattern gives rise to bad relationships, bad communication, bad performance, decision, etc.

(E) **Emotional reasoning** – emotional reasoning refers to a type of thinking pattern where your emotions justify the things in real, albeit the things are not as that in real. You are feeling it because of your emotional perception about you. For example:

(i) I feel guilty; therefore, I must have done something wrong.

(ii) I feel horrible about height. It must be very dangerous on heights.

(iii) I feel disliked. I must really be ugly.

So emotional reasoning is a cognitive process when a person believes what he feels is right regardless of any evidence. For example, from a feeling of jealousy concluding that one's spouse is being unfaithful.

(F) **Should Approach** – should approach refer to a type of thought pattern where you want the things exactly as per your expected way. You want the happenings as per your hope. If it remains less from that level, you feel guilty and low. For example, after presenting a difficult seminar, a bright student said to herself, 'I should not have made so many mistakes.' This made her so frustrated that she quit from presenting for a long time.

Some more examples of should approach:

(i)   I should not eat that much sugar.

(ii) He should not be so argumentative.

(iii) He should not be so rude.

(iv) I should not eat that much.

This should and should not approach does not work usually because it makes you rebellious for resistance, and you feel urge to do that more. For example, if you say 'I should not eat sugar.' It attracts you more to sugar. Dr Albert Ellis has called this 'MUSTerbation.'

How to Watch and Reinstall Your Thought Pattern

Your quality of thoughts is a real magical tool for you that can tremendously change or reshape your life. You should be a constant checker and visitor of your thoughts, work, and be aware like a gatekeeper.

An efficient gatekeeper or watchman always asks the visitor for his identity, his concern to visit, his very purpose to visit, and all. So like this efficient gatekeeper, you also should check. Your each thought, its quality, (negative/positive), its purpose (to harm/to benefit), its effect (to exaggerate/to relief), and then let it allow to sustain it in your mind because you are solely the master of your mind and your life.

Sometimes, slackness happens by chance through watchman, and visitor enables to enter inside without basic inquiry due to emergence of situation. The same happens with mind. You feel or find yourself unable to control or to inquire about the proper relevance of your thought to enter into the mind. The emergence of situation prevails over the quality of thought entering into your mind, and you feel lost in it. Don't worry at all!! You can later on reprogram your mind—it's all in your hand. If the entering quality of thought is disturbing you and your efficacy, if the thought is letting you down from your peace of mind, just take a command in your hand and say, 'This thought is not at all good and beneficial for my mental and physical health. It is ruining my peace of mind; and with the best of my knowledge, my piece of mind is uttermost precious for me. Rest everything else is secondary, so I 'your name' now at once from the moment command you 'the irrelevant thought' to leave my mind and never come again. I strictly order you to get out from my beautiful mind because you are totally garbage. And I am strong enough to let you never visit again in it.

Do it several times in a day and check. You will be very soon free from negative quality of thought. For example, thinking about your wrangle with your friend is upsetting you continuously. And it is not good for your friendship as well as it is disturbing you for your studies and all other peripheries of life. So here you can say, 'I choose to leave this thought from my mind.' I, Aditi Sharma, now at once command my mind to throw out the thinking of quarrel with Arun. I order you, the whole episode of quarrel to get out from my beautiful mind coz you are totally garbage. And I am strong enough to never let you visit again in my mind.

Repeat it three times in a day and night. This little exercise will do remarkable change in your disturbed mental state very soon.

The happiness of your life depends upon the quality of your thoughts. Therefore, guard accordingly and take care that you entertain no notions unsuitable to virtue and reasonable nature.

Generally, people think the way they are behaving is only influenced by external environment or situation. For example, your junior did not obey you, or your friend could not attend you for coffee as per given time.

Moreover, you will become angry or frustrated, and the obvious blame for your anger will be the external reason— disobeying or coming late.

But the hidden truth is in your mind. You are angry because of your own thoughts or projection for you, only triggered by this external situation, so the situation is only the trigger. The content lies within you. Just have a look.

When your friend did not reach on time, your thought might have been like this:

(i) He/she has no values of me.

(ii) He/she always does the same.

(iii) He/she takes me for granted.

(iv) Am I so free, waiting for him/her so long.

(v) Or something and wrong could have happened with him/her.

These all are your own thoughts, eliciting in your mind without knowing the situation and cause objectively.

And these all thoughts are sufficient to grab you in anger, sad, frustration, and despair without realising the truth honestly. The story even didn't end here because you have a preconceived logic for his/her being late. Now on his/her arrival, you will start to argue to prove your point rather than to listen graciously and accept the situation.

The situation becomes worse now, which definitely will be a loss for your mental peace, and eventually, a suffering relationship at last. On the other hand, you might have accepted the situation as it is, and (without any preconceived thought) wait till the real reason be expressed before you. The scenario might have been completely different. The evening you rushed in gloom and anger might have been filled with joy and ecstasies even.

So if you want to sustain a cheerful life, you must have to learn to watch the quality of your thoughts. It is quite tough to overcome or reprogram your quality of reflexive thoughts, which grabs you in anger and despair. Such thoughts seem rudderless and uncontrollable. But this all happened due to a long training from childhood, so don't bother. Have patience, practice, and a constant watch will make you master for the quality of your thoughts.

Next time when any situation will overcome you, just have a pause and ask yourself, 'What made me to think like this? Is this thought beneficial for my mental peace? Am I able to choose something better than this harmful thought?'

Now shift your direction of mind and choose the thoughts that cherish you, spring you think different, live different.

People around us often indulge in the discussions of negativism because it is very easy to hook up on these issues. They say 'there are wars, wrangles, rape, felonies, crime, and massacre, and all where the good at all. This environment is a mess and turbulent place.'

Yes, quite true, but trust me, there is more light in the world. So many people are there who only and only enlighten the candle in the dark. The world is an ultimate lovely place. Don't let you hunk to the critical mass. Just actualize your real potential, create a shift in your mind, and this only life is enough to create a turning point not only for you but for this whole world by you. There is much nobility on the earth, quantum of numbers of people who refuge to live life that prevail over truth, nobility, and honesty.

The life has limitless possibilities, abundance of opportunities, and your limits only starts where you agree to limit you.

To reprogram your thoughts, quality required a precise and constant training on daily basis experiences. Mind is so much engaged in scattered thoughts that it needs some comprehensive training to make a shift in quality of thoughts.

Scattered thoughts or positive thoughts both are the mechanism of thinking and perception, but mind doesn't do the process of thinking and perceiving simultaneously. Thinking is conceptual and perception is the real observation of stimulus in the environment. Quality of thinking depends on the proportion of knowledge about the perception. If perception is there with partial knowledge, quality of thoughts becomes scattered.

Scattered thoughts make mind restless and lead in distress. It affects your overall health (mental, physical, and social).

You become more vulnerable to attract more negatives and hence attributed as a failure!

It is all a mechanism, not a preconceived logic of destiny. So starting from today, change your direction of pricking up the goods from your good vibrate frequencies and be the winner of your life!

'We are what our thoughts have made it, so take care about what you think. Words are secondary. Thoughts live; they travel far.' – Swami Vivekanand

The Science and Thought

'By choosing your thoughts and by selecting which emotional currents you will release and which you will reinforce, you determine the quality of good light. You determine the effects that you will have upon others and the nature of the experience of your life.' – Gary Zukar

'The greatest discovery of my generation is that human beings can alter their lives by altering their attitudes of mind.' – William James.

The power of thought is so strong that it can't be undone. The quality of life not only affects one's life, but can affect the whole society, and it is called Maharishi effect. It was reported in 1976 that 1 per cent of community practised transcendental meditation. The results were so interesting. The crime rape was reduced by 16 per cent on average.

The earlier belief was that life is mostly predetermined, but new researches have shown that the truth is entirely opposite. Your thoughts, perceptions, and attitude directly affect your biology. The more critical and judgmental you are, the more your subconscious mind will convince your body for actions and even for worthlessness.

The state of subconscious mind can't be changed because this state depends on your quality of energy by your thoughts. But a big difference you can create in your life is by your choice of thoughts. Your willing installations of thoughts will always overrule.

Sheldon says, 'You are a living, perceiving, knowing being who is in a body. As an infinite being, there are two things that will determine your fate, choice, and awareness.'

Your thoughts are capable to extending cognitive and physical limits. The quality of thought creates placebo effect in mind, which resultants in expectancies and association between things. These expectancies and learned associations bring chemical and circuitry change in brain. The quality of this change is obvious with the quality of your thought. Sooner, these deliberately chosen mindset or introduced mindset transform in adaptation by body and mind.

For example, when subtle cues in environment trigger thoughts about a predator (placebo/mindset), then the body and mind get physiologically prepared to confront even before the predator comes into sight.

People have significant psychological resources to improve their well-being and performance, but their resources often go unused and could be better harnessed.

Thoughts have remarkable controls over body and mindsets. The quality of your thoughts multiplies and emits the same as you are creating. A very common and life experiencing example I am putting here, Ronald (a man) strongly dislikes Shery (a woman) in his office, and strictly don't want to face her because of her shabby look, dirty and extra clever attitude. Ronald never wants to see Shery, but all the time, Shery remains in his mind because of the constant and stable wish not to see her. Gradually, as time passes, it becomes his dormant state of mind.

Now look at the great power of negativity. Ronald got caught up again and again with the presence of Shery. The more he avoided her, the more she caught him up, and the worst began to happen when she started to view him water, tea, lunch, and all.

It was like as any exponential growth is taking place in between the avoiding of Ronald and presence of Shery. Here, you can know it is the magnetic field created by power of his thoughts that is attracting that woman again and again before Ronald, the man.

This happens in your life every day. The things you avoid most come to you most due to that dormant state of mind you have created by keeping it in your mind. This happening lies in the law of physics. Action—reaction that which we think we create that in actual settings of life. The same Ronald was doing. He ardently gave power to her presence before him.

So choose the quality of your thoughts and keep them in your hand. Let them go and loose the grip if they are annoying, anxious, or depressive; and greet them strongly if they are pleasures, positive, and great like this relevant saying:

'The greatest discovery of my generation is that human beings can alter their lives by altering their attitudes of mind.' – William James.

Live with Attitude of Gratitude

Gratitude is an acknowledgement for your materialistic, abstract, or spiritual assets you have in your life. It consists of a deep sense of gratefulness for all the positive things or strengths in life. These strengths may be related to personal, professional, social, or any other aspect of your life. Gratitude is elaborated as a prized human propensity in each religion that is Hindu, Muslim, Christianity, Buddhist, Jewish, and all.

Being in the state of gratitude is a feeling of love, openness, joy, and peace, and to be fully aware with the divine forces in life. This ecstatic feeling opens the door of your inner sensations and feelings of fulfillment. Attitude of gratitude is a conscious choice to fill the mind with sense of blessings.

> *'Let us rise up and be thankful for if we didn't learn a lot today, at least we learned a little, and if we didn't learn a little, at least we didn't get sick, and if we got sick, at least we didn't die. So let us all be thankful'* – **Buddha**

Having an attitude of gratitude creates a long lasting effect on personality. When you start to be thankful, you develop an attitude to perceive the positives in life. Once it becomes your attitude, it eventually becomes your behaviour. So to be thankful and to appreciate can produce a benchmark in your success story.

Attitude of gratitude also helps to subside your weaker sections of personality like it lessens the hike of anger, impulsiveness, and all. It makes you more calm and contended, so you become more confident. Insecurity of being approved or being rejected also subsides with the attitude of gratitude. It helps you to meet the real you once you start to pick up the things that exist in your life for good. You feel fulfilled and want to earn more and more good to be more grateful for the same. You become a fully aware person about your strengths. According to Cicero, gratitude is not only the greatest of the virtue, but the parent of all others.

Meanwhile, you start to appreciate your worth and accumulations, your magnitude of well being start to raise, your life get to evolve in transformation, and therefore, the magnetic frequencies you emit are sufficient to grab more and more positive in your life.

How to Select Your Grateful Areas

Gratitude is a process to recognize the things you have been blessed with and to express appreciation for all that. To choose the grateful areas of your life is an interesting work if followed on regular realm. You can start right now to feel the difference between the thanksgiving state of mind and the state of mind, which is very neutral and affective.

Let's try and start to think about someone or something to whom you are heartiest thankful without any reservations. That might be your friend, family member, office colleague, little child, your pet, your servant, your watchman, your boss, or that might be your little music boat, ice cream sharing, walking, talking, or shopping with a friend. Just choose and think about it.

Now feel the difference. Do you feel lighter? Expanded? Relaxed? I trust you have! If not yet, then start again and search again the real thing for which you are thankful. Sometimes, it is tough to find out such things because of the conflicted states of mind and due to complex layers of thoughts.

So close your eyes, count your breaths from one to ten, inhale, and exhale. Now slowly, slowly think about that person or that thing what makes you in pleasure, peace, or in pride.

Prepare a wonderful list of gratitude for you as a daily exercise. The daily practice of this list will create a profound difference in your life. Here are some steps to take you further on your gratitude list:

1. **Scroll down the top big five blessings of your life:** Just have a look on your big achievements areas like your family, your teachers, your school, your office, your friends, and so forth. Make a list from all these areas where you feel fulfilled.

2. **Scroll down for more five specific blessings in your life:** This area will make you more specific in choosing the things for you to feel grateful for; for example, your profession, your past, your social image, or your quality of relationship, and so forth.

3. **Scroll down to ten little things as blessing in your life:** Keep tracking for the tiny-miny things that give you momentary pleasures. For example, an evening with your lovely friend, shopping of new arrivals, or

traveling with your best pal, help of a needy one, smile on someone's face due to you, brightening laugh of a child, and the list goes on and on and on. Make a list of your own things that make your moments happy for short period of time. Pay attention to these moments, cherish them, feel them, and start to pay your thanks for these things.

4. **Scroll down your blessing as a person:** Track your personal strengths here. Make a list of at least ten focuses of your attributes such as how you feel about yourself, your will power, your beauty, your intelligence, your communication skills, and so forth. For example, you can prepare your gratitude list as:

   • I am thankful to God to have such a strong will power.

   • I pay my heartiest thanks to you God. You have bestowed me such a good health.

Make your personal attributes list and do a daily practice of thanks to God for these showering. The discussed techniques will help you to search out your grateful areas.

To Whom and How to Express Your Gratitude

• The must and most prize stimulus of your gratitude is the generous God. You always have so many reasons to be grateful to God. You are always surrounded with immense blessings bestowed by God to be grateful for.

- Make your own list of precious gratitude and held it for a thanksgiving time to the almighty. For example, 'God, you have blessed me such a beautiful life of prosperity and happiness. I specifically thank you for this, so humble you are! Thank you God, thank you so much.'

- The next time you feel troubled and sad, track out your top five blessings, consciously write them, transfer your focus on them, and begin to give thanks to God.

- Your next projection of gratitude may be any person at a given moment of time. That may be your mother, your father, sibling, friend, teacher, relative, or even a stranger. Learn to pick up good things and pay thanks for them. For example, if your mother cooks a delicious meal for you, say to her, 'Mumma, you have prepared such a delicious dinner today, thank you. Love you so much for that.'

You can be thankful to your parent, teacher, friend, kids, animals, and even yourself. Be thankful to the people who show you your weakness because now you have the areas to work on with and to grow more.

The regular practice of paying gratitude can change your life immaculately. Various research findings suggest that one simple act of thanksgiving each day may evoke tremendous positive effects in your life: it increases your feeling of happiness, up the level of motivation, induces better sleep, more working out, more kindness and compassion, even it also better your immune system, and you also start to enjoy a contentment in your relationships.

Be Specific to Start a Lifestyle of Gratitude

(i) **Make a true presence in your present:** You cannot truly enjoy the gifts of your life without being aware with the present moments. Make a graceful communication with people, indulge yourself in active listening, and enjoy natural surroundings at the given moment of time. This process of knowing the present will make you more aware about the gifts you have in your life.

(ii) **Love your self:** When you have love for you in your heart, believe your love will never be less for others as well. So learn to love yourself. Be committed with you, recognize your strength, and tap yourself for you. Measure your success and happiness. Your awareness about you will make you perfect in paying gratitude.

(iii) **Examine your will power:** Take one essential test. Track your one instinct for which you feel bound to do. Ask yourself how to measure my will power. Now instruct yourself. For example, I am going to leave my morning cup of tea for five days. Even you can't think to do so. But pick it up with a strong grab and hold it for five days. In the last of the day, tap yourself for your committed act you performed. It will make you ready for next day. Take this five-day power test to check your will power. On the sixth day, you will feel an immaculate change in your strength of will power. You will feel more determined and your level of gratitude will hike up naturally. Prepare yourself for this thanksgiving challenge initiates for a day, then for a week, for a month, and so on, and who knows maybe this challenge will start you to be committed to write down your success story.

Gratitude is not something which sounds good when someone says you thanks, but it is a mindset of positivism that transform your life into happiness. When you practice an interesting episode of paying gratitude on a daily basis, it helps to transform your complaining mindset into a solution-oriented mindset. Even when you have a grateful attitude, people love to talk you, meet you, and your positive energy also becomes contagious for all of them. They even feel miraculously safe in your company. It enhances your general well-being and happiness.

How Attitude of Gratitude Transforms Your World of Perception

Sometimes, it is tough to be grateful when you are in misery. You have lost your job, you have lost your loved one, and you are in relationship wrangle, but your little conscious effort for untouched blessings in your life will create a shift in your state of mind.

For example, Karan is your neighbour but bothers you for one and many reasons. You don't feel any option to get rid of him except to be irritated and all. This state of negativity about Karan is harming your mental health, and consequently, your behaviour. Just do a little exercise here by adopting an attitude of gratitude. Make a list of positive attributes about Karan. Pay attention on Karan's characteristics, his physique, his sparkling laugh, and his witty sense of humour, (which sometimes makes you laugh). Now read this list two times a day and appreciate these traits of him. The more you read this list, the more transformation you will notice in your perception for Karan. You will now be able to draw positives from Karan, only by redesigning your mindset about him by practicing 'attitude of gratitude.'

Sometimes, this little exercise of **Attitude of Gratitude can transform your world, miraculously!**

How to Make it Your Behaviour

More or less, every successful person practices gratitude for blessings in his life. This practice can be your habit too with some little efforts as given below:

- **Journaling:** Write down your blessings for fifteen days, be attentive for your blessings, write them and feel them, and watch the difference between pre and post state of mind.

- **Talking about:** Share your thanksgiving areas with your friends, family, and colleagues. Make it your habit. This habit will multiply your feelings of appreciations and contentment.

- **Searching About:** Be on the attentive mode of searching new and little blessings and happiness in your daily routine. Feel them, write them, and be thankful for them.

- **Practicing:** Prepare your specific and sharp list of gratitude and set your plan for fifteen to twenty days to read it daily in relaxed state of mind, so that it will slowly become your predominating thoughts. More you practice, more your subconscious will be sunk with the incredulous attitude of gratitude.

Do a Self-Test

Do a self-test. How instantly paying gratitude alters your mood.

- Take a scrap of paper

- Write down prayers of your mother for you, she usually do.

- Feel and imagine and feel

- Write down about your laughter with your friends.

- Write down about your best moments you feel.

- Pay thanks to God for everything.

- Visualize and feel everything you have written down.

Now check the difference between your mood pre and after.

I wish and hope you are in a terrific mood now! That's great!

Behold Affirmations

Affirmations are the statements about a perceived truth, and works as a very useful tool in reprogramming of mind. Affirmations are aimed to work on conscious and sub-conscious mind, which resultantly affect the behaviour and action. Affirmations were first come in light by French psychologist Emile Coue back in 1920s. Various researches have proven that affirmation protects against the damaging effects of stress, it boosts the individual's problem solving abilities, mental health abilities, and helps in the development of educational intervention. 'PLOS ONE' (Carnegie Mellon University).

Studies also suggest that constant practice of self-affirmation boost the academic performance in underperforming kids, and effects on actual problem solving performance under pressure.

Affirmation motivates direct and focuses the mind toward the goal you want to achieve. It can work best into believing the stated concept because mind does not recognize the difference between reality and fantasy. For example, while watching a movie, audience get so much identified with the emotions reflecting in movie that their mind perceive it as real, and they start to feel the same emotions, reflecting in the movie. They start to cry, laugh, or love only through the process of identifying with the emotions reflecting in the movie. Another example about mind does not recognize the difference between reality and fantasy is the cricket match. Whether it is practice pitch or real pitch, the mind of the player perceives both the situations as in the real match. The actions and strategy of the player is the same on both the pitches.

In the same way, affirmations are such statements, which help to create reality in your mind for perceive truth if practiced well. Well-studied theory of self-affirmation in social psychology given by Claude Steele contends if individuals reflect on values that are personally relevant to them. They are less likely to experience distress and fear, and react in a balanced way when confronted with adverse situations.

Experimental investigations suggest that self-affirmation can help individuals to cope with threat or stress, and might be very beneficial for improving academic performance, health, and reducing defensiveness (Cohen and Sherman, 2014).

Affirmation and Science

Is there any science behind affirmation? The answer is unequivocally, yes. Researches have shown that affirmations actually change the brain on a cellular level; thoughts have a direct connection to health – Dr Joseph Dispenza.

Neurons tend to connect in brain by thoughts and memories. These thoughts create a pattern or a neutral net. Here's a great example given by Dr Joseph Dispenza.

The feelings of love create a large neural net. Each person builds his/her own concept for this emotion of love. Some people have connected love to happiness and pleasure, so when they think about love, they intently start to experience the memory of happiness and pleasure in meals, which may be linked to a specific person, which then is connected back to love. In other words, brain cells that fire together were together. The more you feel in certain way, the more you develop a long lasting relationship with the same state of mind.

So there is the certain science behind how affirmation works. A new study published in the Journal of Personalities and Social Psychology Bulletin found that people in low position of power may perform better by using self-affirmations to calm their nerves. Proof also says how DNA can be influenced and reprogrammed by words and thoughts. It depends upon the frequencies of thought and statements being what.

This is possible because living DNA (in living tissue, not in vitro) always react to language-modulated ray and even to radio waves. That is why it can be explained that affirmations and autogenous training like are able to have strong effect on mind and body (Pjofr Garjajev).

That contently kicks you to focus on the goal. You start to live in lighter side of vibrations and perceive the truths to be as you are saying. According to Eve Eschner, a relationship expert, Reticular Activating System (RAS) has a major occur for the way affirmations work. RAS works as a filter machine for information. It filters out the information we don't need and filters in the information we need. Without this system, our senses would have been overloaded, and we would go into massive overwhelm.

Declared or perceived truth creates a happening state in mind due to repetitions. Thus, RAS get message that it is very important for you, and RAS get busy in noticing ways to help you achieve your goals. For example, if you want to lose your weight, you will suddenly start to notice the gym and weight loss products and so forth. Meanwhile, affirmation kicks you for high gear.

How Affirmations Work

An affirmation is in a form of a sentence related to some specific goal, interest, need, or desire. These statements are fully drawn in hope to be true. That's why these statements create an awareness and preparedness in mind to become effective in the direction to achieve the goal.

For example, if you are affirming yourself to secure good marks in exams, you suddenly become aware for the related study material, start to prepare good relevant notes, focus on study hours, and you start to remain in a dynamic diffusive state of mind that constantly kicks you to focus on the goal. You start to live in higher side of vibrations and perceive the truth to be as you are saying.

Researches have proven that human mind have between 45000 to 51000 thoughts in a day. Among these thoughts, 70 to 80 per cent thoughts are negative or reckless by various reasons due to learning patterns or genetic influences and all. Out of these thoughts, a major part is on subconscious level, means you are not consciously aware of those thoughts, but these thoughts channelize your behaviour. The science of affirmation teaches how to access conscious and subconscious mind, so that these negative patterns of thoughts can be brought into awareness and replaced by new positive brain circuits and thought patterns. The result is positive, calm, focused, and sharp mind, ready to problem solving, managing life's harsh reality, and creating health, success, harmony, and joy (Phil Shapiro).

Affirmation is the technique through which the quality of these thoughts can be changed. Affirmation is to create believe in one's strengths and abilities. These are the reminders of those believes that you want to live your life with. These reminders are in the form of statements that you say to you or either you listen them.

For example, if you want to be an athlete in running, you can say to yourself, 'my legs are very strong.' If you would repeat this statement again and again for several times in a day, your mind will create to imagine the strong and healthy legs very soon. Certainly, it will be helpful in your running.

Same thing you can do for any short-term or long-term goal in your life, for your presentation before boss, for any important meeting, for such an event where you are in fear of being evaluated, for your health, wealth, and happiness. You can use affirmation for any goal or believe you want to make in your life.

Words and thoughts that are repeated over and over again are regarded by subconscious mind, and therefore, subconscious mind endeavors to align these words and thoughts with reality.

This refers if you often speak or think 'it is tough to survive with honesty.' The subconscious mind will regard and accept your words and put obstacles in your way in becoming honest. On the contrary, if you continued telling yourself that it is great to live life with honesty, your mind will start to find the ways to become honest. So you should be aware while choosing your words for you and others. If you consciously choose the thoughts and words for the quality of your life, soon you will be able to create new situations and strengths in life.

How to Make Affirmations

Affirmation is a potent technique, but it may be impotent for you if not well framed logically. Here are some certain laws in creating effective and healing affirmations:

(a) **Find your goal:** The first and foremost step to create affirmation for you is in knowing your goal. Don't bother how tough or far your goals is. If it exists in real and logical, it will be in your hand. Shift your focus from problem to solutions.

If you are suffering from any disease, focus on health. If you are in fear, focus on bravery and confident state of mind. If you are poor, focus on wealth. If you are failure, focus on success. If you are aggressive, focus on peace, love, and calm. Find your goal precisely to make affirmation for you.

(b) **Affirmation should be simple and short:** Conscious and subconscious mind easily grasp the positive and simple statements and creates mental images soon. So prepare a list of simple and short statements for you. For example, 'I am becoming better and better day by day.' 'I am powerful.' 'I am slim.'

(c) **Affirmation should be in positive form, not the negative:** If you create the affirmation—as 'I am very confident'—the conscious and subconscious mind will create the mental image of confidence and strong because subconscious mind understands only visual, auditory, and sensation. On the contrary, if you say 'I will not get nervous.' Your mind will create the image of nervousness rather than understanding the meaning of the statement because the conscious mind doesn't interpret the meaning. It only see, listen, and feel with the process of visual auditory and sensation. So try to choose your affirmations in positive form, not in negative. For example, 'I am able to do.' 'I am very confident.'

(d) **Affirmation should be specific:** Affirmation should be related to your goal. It should be realistic and logical such as 'I am becoming a wealthy person day by day.'

This affirmation is specific for wealth and logical also, which can be easily sunk by subconscious mind.

(e) **Don't make pressure on you to accept the affirmations:** Speak them or listen to them repeatedly. As soon as you will repeat the statements, your mind will accept them and you will be able to create new believes about you.

How to Use Affirmations

Here are some easy suggestions to use this significant tool to triumph over negative thought patterns:

(a) **Framing:** Make a list of certain positive statements related to specific goal. Such as if you want to get rid of your illness. Frame the statement like this: I am feeling wellness day by day; I am feeling energetic; I am becoming healthy now.

(b) **Practice:** Practice and repetitions are the keyhole to make affirmations effective. Without repetition, there will be no benefit because the deep-seated negative thought patterns are not so easy to change. They need constant effort and regularity to convert into positive thought circuits. The subconscious mind takes time to form the positive thought circuit related to wellness and happiness, so speak the framed affirmations loudly in repetitive manner for three times daily. You can also listen or write these statements for you three times in a day to create a reality in your mind. You can also get a friend or coach or mother or father figure to repeat your affirmations about you.

Don't give up early if you feel affirmations are not working because as deep embedded the negative patterns are, as long time they needed to convert to be reprogrammed. So have patience, and do it with full of your heart.

(c) **Timing:** Affirmations work best when repeated in relaxed state of mind, so the best time to write or listen or think affirmation is just after getting up in the morning and before going to sleep in the night. You can also practice it when confronted with the problem you are suffering from. For example, if you are in anger, practice the affirmation for peace. But you can also practice when feeling serene, calm, and quite. It will help to seat deep this converted thought in subconscious mind fast.

(d) **Faith and Emotion:** Trust and faith is the spine of all wellness, so do this exercise with all your trust, faith, and intensity. Use your focused and creative mind to practice and spiritual exercise.

Affirmation is the best powerful tool to change state of mind or mood to manifest the change you desire in your life. When you say them, think them, or even hear them, they become the thoughts that create your reality. So affirmation can change the thought pattern in positive way if used correctly. Here is the list of some affirmations you can use:

Affirmation for Health

1. 'I am feeling healthy day by day.'

2. 'My mind is becoming calm and peaceful.'

3. 'My body is blessed with beauty.'

4. 'I am feeling strong and energetic day by day.'

5.   'I am taking good care of my body.'

6.   'I am taking good care of my mind.'

Affirmations for Wealth:

1.   'I am growing richer and richer day by day.'

2.   'My income is growing higher and higher.'

3.   'I am becoming more able to attract to money.'

4.   'I am as a magnet for money.'

5.   'I am sensitive and wise in using money.'

6.   'I am becoming rich, richer, and the richest day by day.'

Affirmations for Goal:

1.   'My mind is clear and focused toward my goal.'

2.   'My planning is becoming clear day by day to achieve my goal.'

3.   'I am working hard to reach to my goal.'

4.   'I am growing daily to reach my goal.'

5.   'I am becoming sharp, sharper, and better day by day.'

6.   I am resourceful enough to catch my goal.'

Affirmations for Happiness:

1.   'I am a peaceful being.'

2.   'My mind is full of serenity and happiness.'

3.   'I am enjoying my life with all happiness.'

4.   'I am spreading happiness everywhere.'

5.   'I am celebrating each moment of my life.'

6.   'I am kind, I am loving, so I am happy, happier, and the happiest.'

Use some of these affirmations to enjoy a miraculous change in your life.

'You will be a failure until you impress the subconscious with the conviction you are a success. This is done by making an affirmation which clicks.'

(Florence Scovel Shinn)

Power of Visualization

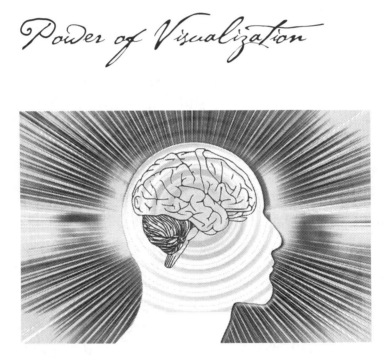

Nothing ever becomes real unlike it is experienced – **John Keats**

In life, everyone aspire to do, own to have great things, wants to live a happy life, want to achieve goals, but only few of all are creating the real happiness and success in life for what they aspire actually. Others only complain for what they have not, they have not enough money, good friends, true relationships, success, romance, joy, and happiness in life.

Finally, they all tend to point fingers on outside factors and develop a blaming attitude on circumstances and on people, which in real make their life more difficult. This mental state yells them in worse and in inefficient web of illusion that others who are on epitome of success have favourable conditions so have grown, but we have not. This makes them poorer and develops strong mental barriers of impossibilities.

In actual, people need to understand that they all can do the same. It is simply to be just strategically and tricky to grab the fortune to live the life of their dream. There are not certain rules or scientific formula to live life of your wants, but have you ever noticed that there are certain common feature that successful people practice and anyone can learn and practice them if owe to learn.

Visualization is one of them, such a mental practice that can help you to reach your goals and wants. Visualization is a mental technique to create images of what you want to have in your life. This is the technique that helps you to focus and direct your thoughts. Visualization is not about that thought that one day you will have, but it is the creative imagination of your goal in here and now. Believe, focus, and act as if you already have your goal. Live with that, feel that, and be thankful for having that as in real.

For example, you want to be a doctor. Believe and focus that you are a doctor. You have a well-equipped clinic filled with patients waiting for you. People are admiring you for your services, and you are feeling blessed.

You can use this technique for anything in life you want to have. This is the mental rehearsal you create the images of whatever you want in life, as if you already have. But remember, this is the rehearsal so repeat it over and over. Students can easily do it for their good examination marks, or as if they have topped the institution or for their career issues. They want to become doctor, engineer, professor, teacher, scientist, politician, and so forth.

What you focus on, you attract that in multiplication. This is your subconscious mind, which enables you to make conscious efforts and to generate energy for what you persistently focus. You can use the technique of visualization in your relationships, in your success deals, in social performances, or with any goal you want to achieve in your life.

Here are some great examples of the success of visualization. Arnold Schwarzenegger, who is a five-time winner of the Mr Universe title, movie star, and a Governor of California himself, used it. Before he won his first Mr Universe title, he walked around the tournament as if he has already won the title; and at last, he won it. He also did it daily as if he has become a successful star and earning enough money.

Visualization is a mental practice, which brings you closer to where you want to be in your life. Numerous examples of remarkable success have proven the power of visualization, such as Natan Sharansky, a computer specialist later on became the world chess champion because of creative mental practices he tend to use in his solitary days during prison for constant years. He tends to visualize himself as a world champion in chess. Miraculously, in 1996, Sharansky beat world champion chess player Garry Kasparon and became the world chess champion.

Various well known athletes like Tiger Woods, world champion golfer Jack Nicklous, heavy weight champion Muhammad Ali employ this mental practice on regular basis for years.

Visualization and Brain

Researches have proven that mental practices create almost same changes as true physical practices—means doing and thinking both affect brain in the same manner. Visualization impacts many cognitive processes like motor functions, sensory function, attention, planning, and memory.

Guangyue, an exercise psychologist, conducted a study on people who went to the gym and the people who carried out virtual workouts in their mind. He found very interesting results. People who go to gym increased 30 per cent of muscle strength, and the people who were mentally trained for weight training got increased muscle strength 13.5 per cent, which is almost half as much of the real workouts.

The power of visualization is to seeing than to believe then to act. If you really want the likelihood of reaching your goals, you should begin it from the practice of visualization.

How it Works

- Visualization works scientifically in helping you to reach your goal. It makes you sharper for your goal. It creates a state of preparedness within you to achieve your goal.

- When you start to visualize your goal in here and now, you are filled with positive emotions like enthusiasm and motivation to grasp your goal as soon as possible.

- The practice of visualization keeps you alien with your actions and efforts toward your goal.

- You become more attached and regular for the strategies to achieve your goal. It keeps you energetic for that is the long run.

- Therefore, visualization promotes your overall thinking in positive to attain your determined goal.

When you think of a big goal that you want to achieve, your brain naturally tend to think many obstacles that will fall apart in between you and your goal. Your brain/mind become defensive for your goal due to these obstacles, and sometimes you get setback rather than to stood affirm and fight for your goal.

Here, the practice of visualization creates a firm picture in your mind about your goal. It makes you more vivid and better. You simply learn to put a positive vision into your everyday life.

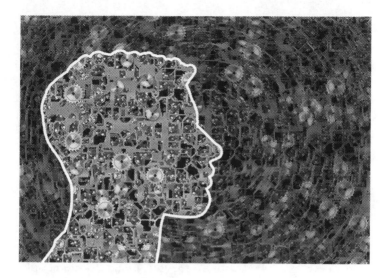

How to Use Visualization

Visualizing will create magic in achieving your goal if practiced precisely with some important key points in mind.

(1) **Be relaxed:** to begin visualizing your goal, you need to be relaxed first. Find a quiet place to sit or lay in relax. Focus on your breathing pattern for few moments, then gently let yourself enter you in your dream as if you are living it now, as if you have already achieved it. Just try to live it and feel the change, enjoy the state of mind you have felt during and after visualization. For example, if your goal is to become an IAS officer or a remarkable administrator, visualize yourself as if you have become an IAS. Just feel the charm and glamour of the post. See yourself sitting on that powerful chair for which you have craved a lot. See you in well-dressed attire

and junior subordinates saluting you. See yourself on height to control law and order among people. Live the moments, try to rejoice.

(2) **Try to use maximum of your senses:** Maximum use of your senses will take you closer to your dream. Your clear envision will increase your craving to achieve your goal ardently, so try to use your senses on a maximum level as much as possible.

For example: If you want to lose 15 kilograms of weight, envision your body shape after shedding off 15 kilograms of weight. See yourself in skin-fit attire. See the colour of your dress. Feel what you are feeling. Listen to the people complimenting you for your hard efforts and a new improved shape you have gained. Feel the feelings after listening to the compliments. Feel, see, and enjoy the pride you want to gain. Smell the environment around you.

Although maximum use of senses is not possible in first attempt of visualization, but practice will make you sharp and filtered for all this. Practice and time will lead you to be able to touch your toes while stretching.

Be a picker of details: it brings you to the next level of your sense. When it is said 'to be a picker of details' means to 'be specific.' *For example,* when it is a matter to see you in new shape, you can be specific here like see your waist in the inches you want. See the design of shirt collar you have worn. See the particular person is complimenting you, so time and practice will make you more specific for details.

Repetition: See the images on your vision board on daily routine make you more perfect and honest in using this technique. It also sharpens you in practicing key points elaborated above, so do it on daily basis. Whether for five minutes only but do regularly, and the key factor is 'live and feel it in now' as it is happening with you in now.

'Visualize this thing that you want, see it, feel it, believe in it, make your mental blue print, and begin to build.' – Robert Collier.

Things to be Cautious While Using Visualization

There are some points for which you should be careful before starting this mental practice. There are some caution points that should be followed and cleared in your mind.

(a) ***Need to be honest and realistic:*** Before visualization, you need to be very honest of your goal. So be clear about it, evaluate your realistic surrounding, and especially be focused with your area of interest, abilities, and capabilities also.

(b) ***Know the difference between visualization and fantasy:*** Visualization is certainly different from fantasy. You can fantasize in any area of interest you want regardless of any visible or invisible boundary. For example, you are flying in the blue sky, you are conquering mountains. These all are the euphoric and fantasizing foals. But visualization is exactly to be authentic, sharp, and crystal for your goal along with your abilities capabilities, interest, and realities. Visualization further inspires to take action and moving ahead with strategic plan to achieve your goal.

(c) *Avoid the negative people around you:* People around you work as the biggest catalyst in actual. If you are surrounded with positive-minded people who motivate and praise you, as well as they themselves are positive in life, try to be with them and avoid the people who doubts on your abilities, goals, and visions. If these people are the friends or family members, you can assertively explain them your vision and plan of action for your goal, so that you will be able to keep them gently aside.

(d) *Have faith in you:* Be authentic, assertive, and faithful for you. Avoid negativism, focus positivism, nourish yourself, acknowledge the ability you have, love the life you are living, and avoid toxic people. Remember one golden rule: everybody can't be happy with you, and who are you to make everybody happy.

(e) *Have patience, change takes time:* You need to have persisting efforts and patience in a long run. Change takes time, but the big distance start from one single small step.

Visualization and Science

Visualization works scientifically because when you create a picture of your wants and goals in your mind and see yourself performing perfectly what you want, you physiologically create neural patterns in your brain. This thought is enough to stimulate the nervous system in the same way as the actual event does.

'So be successful in mind almost guarantees to be successful in outer life.'

'Visualize this thing that you want, see it, feel it, believe in it, make your mental blue print, and begin to build.' – Robert Collier.

'What is now proved was once only imagined.' – William Blake.

Direct and Overall Benefits of Visualization

Practice of visualization not only helps to achieve your goal, but this creative technique makes miraculous changes in your personality.

(a) It makes you more resourceful overall. Whether you are striving for one goal but it affects you as a whole.

(b) It boosts your confidence and motivation, so that you start to perform at your highest in all presentations and areas of life.

(c) It accelerates your health because your mind turns to positivism.

(d) It evokes your subconscious hidden potentials and once that happens, reality conforms to that new perception.

(e) It finally prepares you as a strategic action planner. So as a whole, it transform you within.

Magic Lies in Communication

Communication is absolutely a fundamental value in today's world to a successful life. It creates a connection between people and the world, and people with each other. Without communication, one cannot know the feeling of others and even cannot express his/her own feelings to others at the same time. Communication comprises the ability to interact your thoughts, your ideas, your feelings, and wants to each other and the world around you. So communication can be labeled as that magic pill, which can transform your life to the height of success in the form of happy relationships, comfortable and good organizational settings, creating and shaping in beautiful societies, and lastly, is the form of enduring sense of bliss for oneself. But this magic pill creates magic if one knows how to use it in effective manner otherwise it is enough to rush you in disaster. You can understand it here with the interesting story of a king and his prophet.

A king decides to call some great prophets from his kingdom to have one among them with him for astrological predictions by which the king might be more strategic for the betterment of his kingdom. Many prophets approached the king for this great opportunity. Only two among all were selected for the final interview. Now the king asked the first prophet, 'How would I live long'?

Prophet answered, 'My lord, you would live to see all your son dead.'

The king flew with rage and commands his guards to execute hardest punishment for him. The king then called the second prophet and asked the same question, 'prophet, how would I long live'?

'My Lord,' answered the prophet. 'I am looking you enjoying a so long blessed life that you will outlive all your family.'

The king was filled with joy, appointed, and rewarded this prophet with gold and silver coins. Both the prophets know the truth, but one had communicative tact and skills, while other did not.

So effective communication is critical to successful life. It is the basic human activity and enables us to connect with each other (Michael Langley, 2006).

Just try to move your look on success tycoons, whether entrepreneurs, politicians, educationists, or the life transformers. You will find them all enriched with one common trait, and that is the 'excellence of communication.' They all are the incredulous communicators. They know very well how to put their brilliant ideas in a great manner to the people, and therefore, to the world.

Sometimes, you might have noticed that you really have the best and innovative ideas, but you can't sell them or you are unable to reciprocate them in your personal and professional relationships.

Let's have an example: in a group, there might have been great intellects, academicians, thinkers, but have you ever thought who will be the leader of the group? The leader of the group will be that person who is able to understand and reciprocate the ideas of the group, within the group, and outside the group effectively.

Communication is not only to speak, speak, and speak. It's all about effective and precise speaking, listening, and understanding.

Effective refers here that one should have good words and language while speaking along with comfortable body language, soothing tonality of voice, as well as verbal language should follow the rhythm with your body language like face expressions, hand gestures, body movement, and voice tonality. This everything should be in rhythm, only then it is effective communication.

Precise refers here the content of speaking, your purpose of speaking, and the words chosen to relay that content for target person or group. Your words should be appealing, effective, clear, and congruent, and must have kept all the necessary information regarding the purpose of speaking. Precise also refers to your mode of repetition, whether you are in formal communication or informal. Avoid so much repetition, it lessens your effective deliberation, and it also weakens the interest of the target person or group.

Who is Effective Communicator?

Communication is considered effective when it creates understanding at a large level to the target group or person. So who is the effective communicator?

You are considered an effective communicator when people understand your ideas, messages, and written or verbal words at a large level. According to Shetcliffe, 2004 and Michael Langley, it also means that how the person who is listening understands, responds, and acts within the time frame requested.

Therefore, if you are an effective communicator or not can be judged by the response of your listeners, and by the degree of desired outcomes and changes you want too drawn with your listeners.

Here's the beautiful story of an effective communicator. A blind man was sitting with a pot expecting it to be filled with coins by people. To make this possible, he held up a signboard with some words on it. The words were 'I am blind, please help.'

After reading it, there were few coins in the pot. A man was walking by, dropped some coins in the pot, then took the signboard, turned it, and changed the words. Soon, the pot began to fill up. A lot more people started to drop the coins in it.

Next day, the man who had changed the words came again and see the things. The blind man recognized his footsteps and asked, 'What did you write on my board, which made my pot so filled?' The man said, 'I wrote what you wrote, but in a different way.'

What he has written was: 'Today is a beautiful day, but I cannot see it.'

Of course, both the first and second words were saying the same thing that the man was blind, but the second one was more effective because people thought that they are lucky to have eyes to see.

How to Be an Effective Communicator

Communication is the combination of both verbal and non-verbal expressions. It matters a lot how you relay your ideas, thoughts, feelings, wants, and desires to others. If you are just random with your communication skills, believe you can be at the end of the rope of relationships whether in personal, social, or professional life. So the ability to share your thoughts by words or acts is so important for a successful and happy life. There are no mind readers so you need to say and express your mind to people and the world around you, only then you can grow and prosper in your life beautifully.

Communication skills develop differently in each person due to their environment and surrounding like rearing up practices, family's ability to interact each other, peer group, friends, relatives, professional settings, and so forth. Somebody may be perfect with this magical skill, somebody may be moderate, and somebody may be poor or very dull for the same. But good news is that whether you lie in any category of communication skills, you can upgrade it even more, and you can start to learn it from today and now. Only one little thing is required: the will. 'Where there's a will, there's a way.'

Here are some golden rules for you to focus about effective and precise communication:

(1) **Role of Expressions:** Expressions are the action of making known one's thoughts, feelings, or emotions by verbalism and non-verbalism.

In verbal expression, it includes your words, your language, your way of articulation, your assertion, your tonality, and so forth.

In non-verbal expression, it includes your body language, your facial expression, your eye contact, your hand and body gestures, etc. In sum up, the expressions are the spinal cord of communication, so try to ring some of them on your finger to become the incredulous communicator.

Here are some key points about an effective and precise communication:

(a) **Value of Words:** Words are the great weapon that can bring change in the direction you want. Have you ever been noticed a single word can stir the wholesome emotions whether related to a dark memory or the bright one.

For example: A word like 'failure' or 'loser' in talking to a student or client or any relative of you can trigger his/her worst failure or dismay of his/her life, and he may become defensive with you on that moment.

Words act like a force to pull you in full and actions. Words can bring peace, words can create healing, and words can produce intimacy between nation and the world because careful words are originated from careful thinking. Careful speaking can bring a miraculous change in people's lives whether in their professional or personal life. Good words come from the greater vision (Thomas Moore).

If you speak without awareness and only in reflexology, that is visionless and even reckless, then all that happens is just mess. Usually, negative words leave a long lasting impression on mind, especially on unconscious mind. Often, adults at home speak hurtful words to a child, sometimes in the way to message and correct the child and sometimes in reflex due to their own frustration and problem. But it leaves a worst impact on the child's mind.

Care in speaking to a child, especially by a parent or a teacher, requires a degree of self-possession. It needs an ability to see the change in child's life whether negative/ positive by that word. On the contrary, words of praise can do miracle for the injured ego of anybody. It can lift them up. You should own up the everyday saying opportunities to grow your relationships, and to leave your remarkable impression in other's lives.

For Example: 'I am thankful for what you did for me.' 'I actually needed what you did for me.' 'I am so happy to have you in my life.' 'I am fortunate enough to get a son/daughter like you.' 'I need to say, you are a rocking boss.' 'Thank you for your appreciation, I need that.' Simple and direct words can really make wonder in other's lives. **'Words hurt and words heal.' (Thomas Moore)**

Everyone is in distress and under challenges today. Relationships are on worse in life whether with parent, friends, partners, employee, boss, and so on. But one simple step to them is a soft and lovely word of support. By doing this, you can keep yourself away from language pollution.

Everyone needs words of approval and appreciation no matter how successful or famous he/she is. This is the universal motive to be approved and appreciated. So make yourself believe in power of word—it can hurt or heel.

As Mark Twain once coded nicely: 'The difference between a good word and a right word is the same as the difference between lightening and the lightening bug.'

(b) **Body Language:** A major part of communication depends on your body language. It covers about 53–55 per cent of area of communication. Your eye contact, your hand and arms gestures, your way of nodding, your face expression, all these reveals your level of interest and attention for the targets. Eye contact and facial expressions clearly indicate your interest, attention, and involvement with the target person. The length of eye contacts while talking and listening, the frequency, the pattern, and the blink all matters as well as facial expressions indicate your emotions like happiness, sadness, surprise, fear, anger, etc. That's why the proper use of the body language increases your credibility as a good communicator.

For Example: If you consistently look here and there while talking to a person, the person may obviously interpret that you are not interested in him/her. You are shifty, distracted, or may be I (the target person) is boring you.

Some effective Thumb Rules for Speakers

I.   Try to make balanced eye contact with your target person (not too short and not too long).

II. While talking to a group, make direct eye contact with your audience, but remember to move on left and right with your eyes. Try to focus on different member among audience.

III. When you are listening to someone, try to maintain eye contact for five seconds, and then move eyes to other part of the face. It seems as if you are listening carefully. Do nodding sometimes and etc. to show your interest in the speaker.

IV. If you are in argument, you can hold your gaze little bit long. It will show your strength, but it depends to whom and when you are arguing.

V.   In terms of facial expressions, smile before you speak and try to end with the same.

VI. In terms of whole body gestures, try to be comfortable and relaxed while relaying your thoughts and ideas.

VII. When you meet people for some purpose, always introduce your name with handshake and smile.

VIII. Speak slowly and clearly while communicating with other person, so that they can understand you easily.

IX. You can practice to improve your communication skills by watching good movies, news channels, your favorite speaker, by reading good books, etc.

If you start to follow above rules, certainly you can register remarkable comments in your communication and so on with success in life.

(c) **Tonality of Voice:** Your body language tells the people what you are thinking about them. Like the body language, your tonality of voice has the same importance in deliberation of your message. Approximately 30–35 per cent of your communication depends on the quality of your tonality. For effective communication, you need to be very particular for your tonality. Your tone conveys a major part of your personality, your social class, your demography, your current emotional state, your physical state, and definitely your attitude toward the target person/group. If you follow a monotonous tone, change it by adding some high and low pitch.

For Example: If you always speak very softly, people may interpret that you lack confidence or fear or in drive. If you always remain on high, people may interpret you aggressive, impulsive, and enforced. So be high and deep on important points, and softly go slow on secondary points.

We have an example about tonality: Ronaldo wished Joseph goodnight and he meant it—the stars were twinkling, the night was cold, snowing, and pleasures. But Joseph looked at him, and raising his bushy eyebrows, asked, 'What do you mean by goodnight?'

- Do you wish me a goodnight?

- Or mean that it is a good weather?

- Or do you want me to leave the place?

This extract shows that even a simple greeting like 'goodnight' can be taken in three different ways. Therefore, you need to take great care about your volume and tonality.

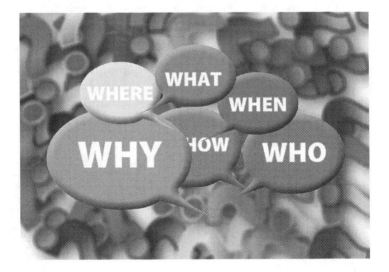

(2) **Be attentive about target person or group:**

One thing should be kept in mind is the ability of the target person or group to whom you want to communicate. The age, ability, nature, intellect of the target person is important when you are in communication with him/her. You can't be same while talking to a child or elderly person, you can't be same while talking with a family member or with your office colleague. You can't be same talking to an academician's group or with a farmer's group, as well as with an illiterate or a literate person.

If you will be same with your way of communication regardless of the abilities or capabilities of the target person, your target person/group will also be very rude to your abilities and capabilities. So it is always necessary to be aware about the limitations of your target group because if only you know what you know, others will think that they know you know nothing.

(3) Mode of Listening

You cannot skip being on listening mode if you want to acquire mastery in communication. Listening is a precious and mandatory slot of effective communication. Your way of listening should be expressive with non-verbal cues: express with your eyes, with you nodding, and if needed, some where with verbal communication.

A listening is only effective when target person realizes that you are getting his/her view. Be engaged in listening. Sometimes, this is the only step you need to take and the problem will resolve.

Listening has tremendous effects in communication; it works like building bridges. When you listen to people, only you don't understand them, but they also understand themselves better. Active listening builds understanding and elucidates you to elicit productive questions.

For example: If you don't understand what the target person means, so you can ask him/her to explain further.

You: Sorry! I don't get your point. Please further explain!

You can practice for your listening ability with anyone around you like a friend, colleague, or your family member. But it should be focused, open, and non-judgemental. Don't fill your listening with your preoccupied harmful sets.

(4) **Worth your questions:** Asking powerful question is an important skill, which works as a strong ladder to take you ahead in life. Asking question also expresses that you are listening actively, so to be a good communicator, try to be an effective question picker.

For example: In relationships or in professional settings, you can ask these following questions after listening to the people properly.

   (i)   'What do you want?'

   (ii) 'What are you going to do for this?'

   (iii) 'How you are going to do this?'

It will be better if your questions are in present form. Remember, asking question is also an art. If you ask question in the present form, you are presupposing the target person.

For example: 'How are you going to do this?'

This question is presupposing your target person that he is certainly going to do something about the issue you are discussing with him. Hence, can be said that your art of questioning can change the mind and can transform the lives. So this is only the communication which exchange and connects, which corrects the wrong, which creates relationships, brings clarity, increases satisfaction in life, removes barriers motivates and exhilarates, and finally helps to know the real you and world around you.

If you understand now the importance of communication, you can further evaluate your own expressions and can take a step ahead to improve more to find success in personal, social, and professional life. As per the saying by famous psychologist Rollo May:

'Communication leads to community, that is to understanding, intimacy, and mutual valuing.'

The Journey Inward (Who Am I?)

*'The first thing you have to know is yourself.
A man who knows himself can step outside
himself, and watch his own reactions like
an observer.'* — Adam Smith

You will have seen most of the time that people talk about each other sometimes about their family members, sometimes about their office colleagues, sometimes about their friends, sometimes about their rivals or enemies, and even sometimes about the person who is nobody to them.

And the content of their talk remains about the criticism of others, the weakness of others, the merit and demerits of others, the faults of others, the quality of others, the strengths of others, the opinion of others, only others and others.

The structural lay out of their talks in some extent remains like this:

A: He is such a clever and selfish man.

B: Ya, I know him for years.

A: Ya, I too, he is like that.

B: Do you know about his son?

A: Oh! No, tell what?

B: Ohhh, very poor conduct tends to wonder here and there. Such a useless chap.

A: Good, his son will teach him lesson, he will fall him in line.

Blah... Blah... Blah...

This all is the scenario of people's daily life. They just create assuming and expectations about others and other's behaviour.

Have you ever noticed that something, the very big, is missing here pathetically? Yes, the missing character here is me, I, I am missing here.

I know others, I always try to know others, but I never try to know me. I actually don't know me.

Who am I?

And the uttermost truth of our life, till the end of it, is that we remain unanswerable for 'who am I' because by childhood trainings and learning, we just become focus on others, who others are, and how they evaluate us. Only their scale of evaluations makes us compatible or non-compatible.

We are rarely taught to know ourselves, to know myself. I am never taught about 'discovery of self.' I am never taught about the pleasure, the ecstasy that I can feel after 'discovery of me.' So I am trained only in discovery of others. But the real truth differs.

'You cannot know others until you know yourself.'

So the real journey of life begins with the search of 'who am I.'

What is Discovery of Self (Who am I?)

In the process of understanding others, we forget what our own life is truly. In knowing others, we become so inkling that we forget to enjoy one of the greatest gifts of life; and certainly, that is discovery of self.

Self-discovery refers here 'to become aware with the way of showing what you are made of.' It provides you the true realization of your version. It is the process of gaining knowledge about your strengths and weaknesses. Your pulse, your true inner voice, and finally, your ringing bells of feelings regardless of the opinion of external world you share (family, friends, or others).

It is all about to know yourself, who you are, an attempt to make in search of your own priorities, values, and character rather than to follow the opinion of others. As Aristotle has said, 'Knowing yourself is the beginning of all wisdom.'

What Is Knowing Yourself?

Knowing yourself is not about to know your surface like your favorite dress or color. Knowing yourself is a process to take you more deep within you. It is an inner journey, a discovery about who you are as a human being—the real you.

Socrates said to 'know thyself.' So this is the process of engagement within self and needs courage to peel back the layers one by one with inside. You will face within the process your worth, talents, strengths, doubts, deep fears, insecurities, and even vulnerabilities bit by bit.

But when we talk about know yourself, the first practical difficulty comes is the ambiguity between me and my behaviour. Remember, your behaviour is not the real you. You are more wide and different. These behaviours are the result of learning patterns or others practices. You are far, far bigger from this.

Here's an example of how your behaviour differ from the real attribute within you:

David, a man who remains in worry always—even he is a worrier—worries about his life, he worries about his children, about his job, even worries about every item on news bulletin, and then worries about what happens next. His family and friends have accepted that he is like this. Even he himself has accepted that he is like this. But it is to be told here frankly that it is not he himself here, but it is just the behaviour he had got used to and needs to be corrected by some concerning expert.

Yes, the underlying cause here to this behaviour may be some deep breed insecurity, so while in the journey of knowing himself, he can reveal it and finally behaviour can be cured too. That's why it is important to question closely whether it is the real you, or it is just your behaviour pattern.

So we can say that self-discovery or self-awareness is the ability to think about yourself and your relationships around you. According to Danil Goleman, 'It is an ongoing attention to one's internal states.' It is the ability to see how your emotions and perceptions are influencing your thinking and than behaviour.

Why it is Important to Know Yourself

At one time or another, each among us dumps in doubts and ask such self doubt questions such as why it's with me only? Why do only I keep having the same problem again and again? Why is it so difficult to handle the people? These difficult but crucial questions propel us to better understand us and then others. If these questions will not be answered properly on some time, we become defensive by denial, blaming, displacements, and regressions.

So to take control over life, it is required to know yourself. It is important because in spite of all things being equal, more people are being undone by behavioural issues than any thing else. Being on the process of self-knowing, you can stop and further can think about what you think, how you think, and hence, why you do what you do.

There is no evidence till yet that any species other than human have this ability of any kind of meaningfulness (why/what). According to Daniel J Siegel, this ability is called 'uniquely human ability.' He says it as essential as our five senses. It allows one to examine closely in detail and in depth about the process by which he/she thinks, feels, and behaves. Although the journey inward is a hard nut to crack, but still, it needed. The leadership expert Warren Bennies writes, 'The most difficult task any of us faces, but until you know you cannot succeed in any but the most superficial sense of the word.'

Know yourself is a creative process. It's not about reaching to destination, it is a comprehensive process where you try to find who truly you are. It is obviously important because the beauty of living consciously increases the likelihood of creating the results you want in your life. Self-knowledge helps you to know your wants and true desires and potentials. Once you are aware with all this, you can further process to work on with these things. It gives you an insight of learning, learning about what you want to work on, and what you want to let go.

According to J Paulsen, 'If you understand how you are most likely to react when things don't go well with you, you can easily identify which thoughts and behaviours are serving you, and those that are not so. The process of self-knowledge creates a deeper understanding within you about your strong and freaky guts, so you learn to relate your value to the world.'

It precisely helps you to move to the place of self-acceptance and self-worth due to the process of acknowledging yourself. You get your perfection and imperfection in your fist. Now you can choose the option here: you can be totally okay with everything or you can change.

The ultimate goal of any life is to attain happiness and peace of mind, whether by doing efforts for your acknowledged goals or by wondering here and there in streets. It's up to you, it's your choice of happiness, and how you are going to make it happen for you. But the key question is: if are you really aware with the area of your happiness, or are you just trying to find it by following the opinions of your family, friends, and society?

Here, that's why knowing yourself is important and crucial for your choice of life. Wandering along with many paths and dabbling in various interests is not going to make you happy. You need to sit and take an introspective look to identify your strength and interest in order to keep strengths in the long run of life.

Happiness, joy, and satisfaction are more easily attained when you are able to use your true strengths and control your flaws in the cause of the goal you believe in. Each person is uniquely talented and has the greatest capacity to grow and develop in the acknowledge area, but it happens when he/she is engaged in work that allows him/her to utilise his/her respective strengths and abilities.

A great saying by **J. Paulsen**, 'The cost of not following your heart spending the rest of your life, wishing that you had.'

That's why it is important to understand who you are, what you are good at, and at what your hair stand up on end hold lessons.

It is certainly useful to your family and friends, and therefore, society because when you understand yourself better, you understand others even better. *'The more you know yourself, the more patience you have for what you see in others.'* — Exile Erikson

Knowing yourself is especially good to keep healthy relationship whether in personal, social, or professional life. When you start to know your strengths, then you also start to relax other's weaknesses. You start to be empathic; your area of affection for people starts to grow rather than the area of perfection from people. You start to accept the people as they are and increase your own capacity to adapt and grow. Seeing your affection and adaptation for them, people also start to adapt with you.

Now here develops a chain of affection and then perfection. But it all starts from you 'with knowledge of the self within you.' So this is why knowing yourself is important.

> *'The better you know yourself, the better your relationship with the rest of the world.''* —Toni Collette.

How to Start the Process of Knowing (Who Am I) Yourself

As it is tough to know yourself, still it needs, so how to make this difficult path some easy and commendable is a strategy. It is a learnable skill that with some direction and efforts, and surely by time can be done better, it is not an all or nothing proposition but a continuum—an ongoing process that you engage in throughout of your life. The choice is up to you. How far you are ready to go with the process, how willing you are to put of the layers bit by bit.

> 'The most difficult thing in life is to know yourself.' —Thales

But most of the people get tired so soon, unfortunately, and just sit back to quit. People have the default way of thinking, and due to their existing belief system, it gets tough to come out from that because they have developed their comfortable zone with that even it seems to them natural from birth.

Part of the problem is your propensity to fool yourself. It is a willful blindness. Socrates had reminded his audience that 'self-deception' is the worst thing of all. In other words, it can be said that a man can't even trust his own mind because mind becomes incapable of seeing things in a complete, honest, and straightforward manner. He hides things from himself, finally reaches in denial and blaming, which is the leading cause of lack of self-awareness. It is then an ever-present force that thwarts your ability to see yourself as you are. After all, when you find the person who you are, you might not like the person you find.

Professor Richard S Tedlow says that denial creates the ignorance of the obvious because you don't want to confront the reality, and further denial creates irrational behaviour of its own. So it's only self-knowledge through which you can be open to criticism and receptive to facts and perspective that challenge your own.

But of course, it is easier to say than to do, and requires a special will and quality and technique that does not come naturally so efforts needed crucially. There are some easy and doable techniques to lead you to the journey of who am I, the journey inward.

(1) **Acceptance with Humility**

The journey inward or knowledge of self is certainly impossible without acceptance (self or other) for which humility is an essential key, which helps you to acknowledge your limitations, problems, and faults. It works as the lubricant to overcome the friction created by 'how we want to see ourselves' and 'how we really are.' It allows accepting the reality that you have limitations and weakness. The apostle Paul says, 'If anyone thinks he is something when he is nothing, he deceives himself.'

So definitely, you need a humble frame of mind and acceptance to learn to make change possible. Humility is accepting how you actually are today. It starts to open up the bud of self-knowledge. It teaches you to face your pains and faults without trying to escape from them. It saves you from denial and blaming attitude. It is like that. How can one be free from prison until he accepts he is a prisoner.

In the same way, humility allows you to accept you first and so others, it allows you to seek solutions for your problems further. So it gives you the patience, tolerance, and understanding, which are mandatory to begin your self-healing and further growth.

Humility is the first step to reduce your egoism, so you start to relate better with self and so on with people. It increases the quality of relationship because humble people accept the people of who they are. Davis says it helps to repair relationships and build stronger bonds between people.

Humble people are better in self-control, helpful, and lastly, they create excellence in leadership of life. When you are humble with your faults and accept them, learning starts to grow from here. You become an opportunistic even in your failings like grains of sand around which pearls can be made grow. So start your inward journey today from the sweet taste of humility.

Look Inward or Introspect

Introspect is a method through which a person look within about his beliefs and about his mental states. The right introspection is when you know to just be yourself and when to step outside yourself to examine your tendencies. In actual, introspection is a process or a method itself to know truly about you. In today's time, you are wrapped in such a world where you can rarely give yourself time in solitude to pamper yourself. From the moment you open your eyes in the morning and even in sleep, the plague of thoughts about external world remains on in your head. But a willful effort to hit downside and think about your own core values, wants, strengths, and weaknesses can make you a truly wise person. As Lao Tzu said, 'Knowing others is intelligence, knowing yourself is the true wisdom. So if your action and thought will be aligned, you can do incredible.'

To introspect, the following steps can be done anywhere, but best if practiced in solitude and on daily routine:

Create Serene and Quiet Space: Serenity and quietness can be in different forms for different people. It can be a long walk along on your own, it can be a sitting in a chair with slow and deep breathings, and it can be a cup of coffee in your favourite cafe house. For some, it can be an extra lying in bed for minutes, so decide and choose your own one. But the crucial think is to make sure that no one is going to disturb you. If you have lack of time no matter, just do it for 15–20 minutes only, but try to grab it for you. Make it your habit on daily routine and better to follow at the same time on the same place. It will help you immensely further in your life.

Practice Self-Relaxation: Once you have created your space, start some self-relaxations here. Feel it is very peaceful (my mental piece is primary, rest everything else is secondary in the world), take slow and deep breaths, focus only on your breaths, count them, in and out, feel them, and let the sensation full you into a relax state. Once you are relaxed, now you can go for explorations.

Journaling with Some Exploratory Questions: You can now on the switch to know your inner self by asking or choosing some open-ended and interesting questions from you like:

- What do I truly want from life?

- What is my deepest passion?

- What I truly desire to do?

- Am I doing that really, if no, why?

- What is my biggest strength?

- What is my weakness, which makes me out of self-control?

- Is it needed to be correct?

- What are my deepest values?

Here, exploration starts to know you. These types of questions are enough to get you start. Further, you can start to craft your own. Here is a further list 1.1 of some questions in the chapter for digging your inner self.

Be Honest and Non-Judgmental: Now this is the turn to be really courageous. You need to be honest with yourself while knowing the answers within you for your explorations.

Ask, Confirm, and Accept: To accept yourself within really needs courage. Self-acceptance and facing issues honestly give you the opportunity to uncover the underlying truths layer by layer. But make you sure for honesty and have non-judgmental analysis to your potentials and weaknesses. If this is your first time doing, you may be shocked or amused with what you find. So don't judge whatever comes out, it is all a part of you.

For example: If you asked yourself a question 'what I am doing this time in my life, is it really my nerve?' If the answer is in no, you may be shocked and somewhere, you may start to deny. So here you really need courage, courage of acceptance to you as you are in real. Once you started to accept yourself enlighten begins. So keep your eyes open non-judgmentally and confront the realities. Enjoy the ride and hold the space and believe 'the new better one will come out.'

Writing: What you are exploring about self, having that in your favourite diary is also very important in the process of introspection. When you write about your reflection, it gives you an extra insight and sharpness about you. It gives you a feeling of continuity, and makes clear track to look back on your reflection. Even it will surprise you more when you read it. So try to write down your strong and weak nerves to transform your inner world.

Except writing answers for your questions, try to write down about your favourite and painful experiences, your childhood memories, and write down the feelings for those experiences too. Writing your daily experiences also allows you to wide awake for your journey inward. It creates a feeling of friendship with your own stuff.

As Eleanor Roosevelt says, 'Friendship with oneself is all important because without it, one cannot be friend with anyone else in the world.'

Find a Mentor: Though only you know for what your heart beats, but still, somewhere you can find yourself resourceless and confused. Having a mentor will be an incredible catalyst for you here when you need to come out from those bumps in the journey of self-knowledge.

So seek out someone to whom you trust, have a definite sense of self. Let your mentor know about the process you have started. He/she can let you know your strength as a guide, and as well as can make you trickier about the milestone of life. You can have more than one mentor in your life, but observe them objectively as much as you can, observe how they are as they are, what special has made them who they are today.

Remember, when you start a different journey, you definitely will need a support system. But most of people don't understand your journey and can brush off in your process.

So here, your mentor will surely help you to screen out again. That's why mentors are crucial in helping you to connect the dots between your abilities, potential, goals, and your success. They provide you the advice, confidence, insight, awareness, and the network that allows you to kind your avenue of success. Here is an eye-opening story to show how having a mentor is really important:

A rabbi gathered together with his students and asked them, 'How do we know the exact moment when night ends and day begins?'

'It is when standing some way away and you can tell a sheep from a dog,' answered one student.

The rabbi was not okay with the answer. Another student replied, 'No, it is when standing some way away, you can tell an olive tree from a fig tree.'

Rabbi again was not contended with it. 'Well, what is the right answer?' asked the students.

The rabbi answered finally, 'When a stranger approaches and we think he is our brother, that is the moment when night ends and day begins.'

So this is the insight an extra awakening in life, which can only be introduced by a true mentor.

Embrace Your Inner Self and Start to Work for Change

When you will be on the journey of 'knowing yourself,' certainly you will get surprises and amusements, but remember it is not wrong or right. There is no such thing as a mistake when you are brushing out of prison. So whatever you face is for your greater good, and definitely a learning opportunity for you. Embrace with self blessings and humility and start to work on daily routine to reap the massive rewards of self-knowledge.

Constant effort, practice, and patience will make it a ring of your finger so remember, we all have power to do but among us very less have desire to do.

> *'Your own self-realization is the greatest service you render the world'* — Ramana Maharishi

EXERCISE 1.1: Self-Exploratory Questions:

Here is the list of thirty one more questions that will open the door of your true inner self. It is meant to help you to discover your habits, your strengths, your weaknesses, your nature, and your interests. There is no right or wrong answer. It is just an effort to get your true reflection.

1. What is your all-time happiness passion?

2. What is that you like to do even after tired up?

3. What do you fear most in your life?

4. What is your biggest strength in life?

5. Who is taking most of decision of your life? You, your circumstances, or the people around you?

6. How do other people understand or perceive you?

7. How do you understand or perceive yourself?

8. What is the difference between both the perception of others for you, and the perception of you for you?

9. What are the things you are grateful for in your life?

10. If money is not compulsion, what would you do in life?

11. On what do you get out of control, and why?

12. What is your biggest weakness? Do you really want to work on with it?

13. If you die tomorrow, how and why people are going to miss you, what they will keep in your eulogy?

14. If you die tomorrow, will you be satisfied with the life you have lived?

15. What was your last act of kindness and when?

16. How much time do you spend on unproductive activities like watching TV, gossiping, leg pulling, or on social media profiles?

17. What is your dream life, and what you are doing to accomplish it?

18. Choose ten words to describe the real you?

19. What are your strengths 1 to 5?

20. What are your flaws 1 to 5?

21. Who are your role model, mentor, and moral support in life?

22. With whom you forget the clock/time.

23. What is your unique ability that makes you special?

24. Who are the people you don't want to spend time with?

25. How do you feel with your failure?

26. What lessons have you learned from your failures?

27. How you are in relationships?

28. What do you want from relations?

29. Do you excuse or forgive people in relationships?

30. Are you a better person today from last year of the same day?

31. What the change you are creating here in the universe as a human?

The journey of the answers of above questions will certainly help you to reach your inner most window to jump in your 'discovery of who you truly are.'

Bibliography

Angie Le Van: (Dec. 03, 2009). Seeing is Believing: The power of visualization, *psychology today*. Retrieved on August, 2, 2015 from www.psychologytoday.com

Atasoy. ozgun (Aug13, 2013). Your thoughts can release abilities beyond normal limits, *Scientific American.*

- Brian Cavanaugh (2004). T.O.K. The Sower's seeds. Retrieved on 13.08.2015 from www.amazon.com

- Burns, David D. (1989). *The feeling good handbook: using the new mood therapy in everyday life.* New York: W. Morrow, ISBN 0-688-01745-2.

- Chakraborty. R, (2015). How you can change your life by thinking: the science behind the power of thought. Retrieved on may 02, 2015 from yourstory.com

- Cicero, M. Tullias 'Gratitude', www.brainyquote.com

- Cohen, G.L. & Sherman, D.K. (2006). "The psychology of self defense: Self-affirmation theory." In M.P. Zanna

(Ed.) *Advances in Experimental social Psychology* (Vol. 38, pp. 183-242). San Diego, CA: Academic Press.

- Coue, E. (1992). "Self mastery through conscious Autosuggestions" Page 19.

- Daniel Goleman (1995).Emotional intelligence: Why it cam matter more than IQ.

- Daniel J. Siegel (2010). *Mind sight, the new sight of personal transformation,* Bantam (first published) January 2009, ISBN: 0553804707.

- David, J. Creswell, Janine M. Dutcher, William M.P. Klein, Peter R. Harris, John M. Levine (2013). Self-Affirmation Improves problem – solving under stress. *Plos One,* 8(5): C62593.

- Davis, M. (2012). Repairing a broken relationship. Retrieved on August, 10, 2015 from www.hubpages. com > relationship problem and advice.

- Dispenza, J. (2012). Inspirations: Breaking the Habit of Being Yourself. Retrieved on August, 9, 2015 from www.gaia.com.

- Ellis, Albert (2014). "Must erbation" is bad for your mental health. *The psych Scrivener.* EDT by Lisa.

- Eschener. E.H. (2011). "Affirmations: Why they work and how to use them". Retrieved on Sept., 9, 2015 from www.spiritualityhealth.com

- Gary Klein (2013). "Seeing what others don't. The remarkable ways we gain insights" New York, NY: *Public Affairs,* ISSN 978-1610392518.

- Gary Zukev, Gary Zukev quotes, Love heals community.

- Gregory Alford, 'self care'. Retrieved on August, 13, 2015 from http://www.acceleratedcoaching and consulting.co.in

- Guang Yue (Nov. 21, 2001). "Physical training in your dreams" you are in: Health, BBC News.

- Hanson. R (2015). Just one thing: forgive yourself greater good, the science of meaningful life. University of California.

- Howard Gardner (1998). *Extra ordinary minds*, Basic Books, Malayshia. ISBN: 0465021255.

- John Kehoe (2015). Mind power 1997, Zoetic Inc.

- John Raithel, 'Three types of thoughts'. Retrieved on August, 17, 2015 from www.rahul.net/raithel/otfw/three types of thoughts.

- Kevin Wood (Aug. 2013). "The lost Art of Introspection: why you must master yourself. Retrieved on August, 20, 2015 from www.expertenough.com

- Langley, Michael (2006). Retrieved on September, 1, 2015 from http://michael.langley.id.au/blog/psts/37

- Margarita Tartakovsky, M.S., Editor, 30 journaling prompts for self-reflection and self-discovery, Psych central. Retrieved on August 17, 2015 from http://blogs.psychcentral.com/weightless/about-margarita-tartakovsky/

- Marshall Goldsmith (2007). What got you here won't get you there. Retrieved on September, 4, 2015 from, *www.amazon.in/ - What Got-Here-Wont-There/dp/1401301304.*

- Michael Mckinney. Retrieved on September, 2, 2015 from www.michael.mckinney@visionjournal.org

- Moore.T (2011). The power of language. *Resurgence & Ecologist.* NO. 1120414.

- National science foundation, Thoughts. Retrieved on Sep 04, 2015 from www.mind-sets/com

- Neff Kristin. (May 03, 2014). "The importance of self-worth". Retrieved on August, 18, 2015 from http://www.psychalive.org/self-worth/

- Paul Apostle, "If anyone thinks he is something". Retrieved on August, 22, 2015 from http://biblehub.com

- Paulsen, J. (2013) "The cost of not following your heart". Retrieved on August, 21, 2015 from www.blog.zerodean.com

- Pjotr Garjajev (2011) "Scientist proves DNA can be reprogrammed by words and Frequencies, Collective-Evolution.com

- Richard S.Tedlow, Denial (2010). Why business leaders fail to look facts in the face –and what to do about it. Retrieved on August 02, from michael.mckinney@ visionjournal.org

- Shapiro, P. "Affirmations: The power of thoughts. Retrieved on August, 14, 2015 from www.philipshapiro. com

- Sheldon.C.M,(2015). You are a living perceiving knowing being, retrieved on Sep 18, 2015 from http:// prezi.com/.../

- Shetcliffe, John (2004). Managing Regular communication, *Insurance Brokers' Monthly and Insurance Advisor, Lyc,* Vol. 54, 4; Pg. 18, 3 pgs.

- Steele, C.M. (1988). The psychology of self-affirmation: Sustaining the integrity of the self. In L. Berkowitz (Ed.) *"Advances in experimental social psychology"* (Vol. 21, pp. 261-302). San Diego, CA: Academic Press.

- Sumitha Bhandarkar (2013). Retrieved on August 18, 2015 form www.afineparent.com

- Travis Bradberry and Jean Greaves ((2009). *Emotional Intelligence 2.0.,* Talent Smart, ISBN: 978-0-9743206-2-5.

- Warren Bennis (1989). *On becoming a leader*, Reading, Mass: Addison-Wesley Pub. Co.

- Wilson, Timothy D. (2002) "Strangers to ourselves! discovering the adaptive unconscious". Belknap press of Harvard University Press. ISBN 978-0-674-00936-3.

- www.brainyquote.com

- www.goodreads.com/

- www.spaceandmotion.com

- www.wisdomquotes.com

- www.lifehack.org

- www.quora.com

About Anita Moral

Dr. Anita Moral is one of the renowned psychologists in India. She is giving her services towards nation and society as an Assistant Professor in Dr. Bhim Rao Ambedkar University, (Agra, U.P) India.

She is an incredulous Life Coach from International Coach Federation. Her best areas of expertise are parenting and mental health. She is the trained Clinical Hypnotherapist and NLP expert. She is visiting guest for various news papers and radio channels for her expert's views and suggestions. Dr. Moral has more than dozens of research papers and articles in various national and international refereed journals, magazines, and news papers. She is in high demand as a speaker, on 'success and happiness in life', 'positive parenting', and on 'mental health' issues in various schools, colleges, universities and different NGOs across the country.

She has a keen interest and empathic golden heart for children and for the rights of women. Therefore, she has done a first empirical major research project in India on "Attitude towards honour killing and violence against women".

Dr. Moral's personal purpose for life is to help people to live life of their dreams, to help them to find their true purpose of life and to help them in recognize who they truly are. Through her own Foundation "The Moral Foundation" she is helping underprivileged children and women to stand up in their life.

For more information on Dr. Anita Moral please visit,. dr.anitamoral@gmail.com.

Printed in the United States
By Bookmasters